No. 6 **Gray Barker's Newsletter** 1976

APRIL MAY JUNE

Gray Barker's Newsletter
No. 6 (April,May,June)1976

Gray Barker
Alfred Steber (Editor)

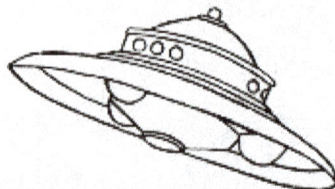

SAUCERIAN PUBLISHER
Original Sources in Ufology

ISBN: 978-1-955087-47-6

9 781955 087476

2023, Saucerian Publisher

PROLOGUE

It is generally a good idea to return to the classics in any genre. This also goes for UFO literature. Rereading a book, or reviewing old documents after ten or twenty years is a rewarding experience. You will discover new data and ideas you didn´t notice before. The reason, of course, is that you are, in many ways, not the same person reading the book the second or third time. Hopefully you have advanced in knowledge, experience, intellectual and spiritual discernment. A good starting point is to reread the UFO classics in order to understand the deeper mystery involved in what happened during that era.

Gray Baker's Newsletter was a leading forum for personal experiences relating to UFOs, psychic abilities, ghosts and hauntings, cryptozoology, alternative medicine, and Fortean phenomena for a devoted readership worldwide. This title is an authentic reproduction of the *Gray Baker's Newsletter* for April,May,June, 1976. Great, but unpretentious, this issue is an extraordinarily rare symbol of what was going on in those early years of the modern UFO phenomena. Cover illustration: James W. Moseley on a balance while Walter Andrus, Director of MUFON, watched.

Saucerian Publisher was founded with the mission of promoting books in Science Fiction. Our vision is to preserve the legacy of literary history by reprint editions of books which have already been exhausted or are difficult to obtain. Our goal is to help readers, educators and researchers by bringing back original publications that are difficult to find at reasonable price, while preserving the legacy of universal knowledge. This book is an authentic reproduction of the original printed text in shades of gray. **IMPORTANT**, despite the fact that we have attempted to accurately maintain the integrity of the original work, the present reproduction may have minor errors beyond our control like: missing and blurred pages, poor pictures and readers' pencil markings from the original scanned copy. Because this book is culturally important, we have made available as part of our commitment to protect, preserve and promote knowledge in the world.

This book has been formatted from their original version for publication. **IMPORTANT, although we have attempted to maintain the integrity of the issues accurately, the present reproduction could have blurred pages and poor pictures due to the age of the original scanned copy.**

Editor
Saucerian Publisher

Flying Saucer Investigator Gray Barker (May 2, 1925 – December 6, 1984)

Gray Barker Grave Site

Grayson R Barker

in the U.S., Find a Grave Index, 1600s-Current

Want to get involved? Click here.

Report a problem

Detail Source

Name:	Grayson R Barker
Gender:	Male
Birth Date:	2 May 1925
Birth Place:	Braxton County, West Virginia, United States of America
Death Date:	6 Dec 1984
Death Place:	Braxton County, West Virginia, United States of America
Cemetery:	Barker Cemetery
Burial or Cremation Place:	Sutton, Braxton County, West Virginia, United States of America
Has Bio?:	Y
Father:	George Elliott Barker
Mother:	Rosa Lee Barker

Photo added by R.C.

Grayson R "Gray" Barker

BIRTH	2 May 1925 Braxton County, West Virginia, USA
DEATH	6 Dec 1984 (aged 59) Braxton County, West Virginia, USA
BURIAL	Barker Cemetery Sutton, Braxton County, West Virginia, USA
MEMORIAL ID	181460934 · View Source

SHARE SAVE TO SUGGEST EDITS

MEMORIAL PHOTOS 5 FLOWERS 3

Gray Roscoe Barker WWII Draft Card

Form Approved
Budget Bureau No. 33-R012-42

REGISTRATION CARD (Men born on or after July 1, 1924, and on or before December 31, 1924)

(Also for the registration of men as they reach the 18th anniversary of the date of their birth on or after January 1, 1943.)

SERIAL NUMBER	1. NAME (Print)			ORDER NUMBER
W 159	Gray (First)	Roscoe (Middle)	Barker (Last)	11,688

2. PLACE OF RESIDENCE (Print)
(Number and street): —
(Town, township, village, or city): Riffle
(County): Braxton
(State): W. Va.

[THE PLACE OF RESIDENCE GIVEN ON LINE 2 ABOVE WILL DETERMINE LOCAL BOARD JURISDICTION; LINE 2 OF REGISTRATION CERTIFICATE WILL BE IDENTICAL]

3. MAILING ADDRESS
Glenville, Gilmer Co., W. Va.
(Mailing address if other than place indicated on line 2. If same, insert word same)

4. TELEPHONE	5. AGE IN YEARS	6. PLACE OF BIRTH
	18	Riffle (Town or county)
(Exchange) (Number)	DATE OF BIRTH: May (Mo.) 2 (Day) 1925 (Yr.)	W. Va. (State or country)

7. NAME AND ADDRESS OF PERSON WHO WILL ALWAYS KNOW YOUR ADDRESS
Mr. G. E. Barker, Riffle, W. Va. (father)

8. EMPLOYER'S NAME AND ADDRESS
None

9. PLACE OF EMPLOYMENT OR BUSINESS
(Number and street or R. F. D. number) (Town) (County) (State)

I AFFIRM THAT I HAVE VERIFIED ABOVE ANSWERS AND THAT THEY ARE TRUE.

DSS Form 1 (Rev. 11-16-42) 16—21630-4 (OVER)

Gray Barker
(Registrant's signature)

Gray Barker's one page FBI File # 157-HQ-3 Serial 6

GRAY BARKER
P. O. BOX 2228
CLARKSBURG, W. VA.

Anti-Jewish Outbreaks-Gen.

January 30, 1960

J. Edgar Hoover, Dir.
Federal Bureau of Investigation
Washington 25, D.C.

Dear Mr. Hoover:

Leon Davidson, of 64 Prospect St., White Plains, N. Y., has sent me a copy of a letter written to you under date of January 13th, expressing concern over the outbreak of apparent Fascist activity, and suggesting some sort of world-wide organization behind this movement.

Mr. Davidson, like myself, has written and published material about "Flying Saucers," and the people he refers to are known generally as belonging to the more or less "crackpot" fringe surrounding those who have tried to investigate the subject seriously.

While I would not want to go as far as Mr. Davidson, in suggesting a sinister organization behind or connected with these people, I do know that some of the writings and literature connected with these fringe groups have contained the "hate" line identified with the Nazis or Fascists.

I certainly hope that the amateur flying saucer investigating field, of which I am a participant, does not become identified with the ideas of some of these minority groups in our field.

While I really doubt that I could be of any real help to you, any of my files certainly would be open to you in helping to cope with this situation of which any citizen should be rightfully ashamed.

I might add that to my best knowledge, none of the saucer fringe groups are tainted with anything which could be described as overtly following the Communist line.

Very truly yours,

Gray Barker
Gray Barker

REC-35 157-3-6

FEB 19 1960

EX. - 131

Not acknowledged due to nature of letter - not [illegible] due to fact Barker has numerous 65 ref.

File

No ack 2/18/60

1 FEB 25 1960

Gray Barker (May 2, 1925-December 6, 1984)

The most famous Ufologist in history, and flying saucer investigator who was the leading figures among flying saucer researchers, who hase challenged the government denial that saucers come from outer space, have been silenced, Gray Roscoe Barker (May 2, 1925-December 6, 1984) was born in Riffle, Braxton County. He grew up in Braxton County and spent most of his life in central West Virginia. After receiving a B.A. from Glenville State College in 1947, he taught school and became a booking agent for theaters in the area.

In 1952, he was working as a theater booker in Clarksburg, West Virginia, when he began collecting stories about the Flatwoods Monster, an alleged extraterrestrial reported by residents of nearby Braxton County. Barker submitted an article about the creature to FATE Magazine and shortly afterward began writing regular pieces about UFOs for Space Review, a magazine published by Albert K. Bender's International Flying Saucer Bureau.

In 1953, Albert K. Bender abruptly dissolved his organization, claiming that he could not continue writing about UFOs because of "orders from a higher source". After pressing Bender for more details, Barker wrote his first book, They Knew Too Much About Flying Saucers, published by University Books in 1956.[4] The book was the first[3] to describe the Men in Black, a group of mysterious figures who, according to UFO conspiracy theorists, intimidate individuals into keeping silent about UFOs. Barker recounted Bender's alleged encounters with the Men in Black, who were said to travel in groups of three, wear black suits, and drive large black automobiles, usually Cadillacs. In 1962, Barker and Bender collaborated on a second book entitled: Flying Saucers and the Three Men. Published under Barker's imprint, Saucerian Books, this book proposed that the Men in Black were extraterrestrials.

Barker published his best-known book, They Knew Too Much About Flying Saucers, in 1956. At various times Barker published flying saucer magazines and newsletters. Through these publications, he contacted people worldwide interested in UFOs, many of whom claimed to have been contacted by aliens.

Over the following decades, Barker continued writing books about UFOs and other paranormal phenomena. In 1970, following the 1967 collapse of the Silver Bridge in Point Pleasant, Barker published his next book, The Silver Bridge. This publication is related to the famous legend of the Mothman sightings. Although he published many other books on strange phenomena, Barker is best known for these two books and a 1983 publication called MIB, *The Terror Among Us*, about the Men in Black. He was the subject of the 1995 video by Ralph Coon, Whispers From Space. For this production, Coon collected stories from various people who knew and worked with Barker.

Though his books advocated the existence of UFOs and extraterrestrials, Barker was privately skeptical of the paranormal. His sister Blanch explained that Barker only wrote the books for the money, and his friend James W. Moseley said Barker "pretty much took all of UFOlogy as a joke". In a letter to John C. Sherwood, who had submitted materials to Saucerian Books as a teenager, Barker referred to his paranormal writings as his "kookie books."

Barker occasionally engaged in deliberate hoaxes to deceive UFO enthusiasts. In 1957, for example, Barker and Moseley wrote a fake letter (signed "R.E. Straith") to self-claimed "contactee" George Adamski, telling Adamski that the United States Department of State was pleased with Adamski's research into UFOs. The letter was written on State Department stationery, and Barker himself described it as "one of the great mysteries of the UFO field" in his 1967 Book of Adamski.

According to Sherwood's Skeptical Inquirer article "Gray Barker: My Friend, the Myth-Maker", there may have been "a grain of truth" to Barker's writings on the Men in Black, in that the United States Air Force and other government agencies did attempt to discourage public interest in UFOs during the 1950s. However, Barker is thought to have greatly embellished the facts of the situation. In the same Skeptical Inquirer article, Sherwood revealed that, in the late 1960s, he and Barker collaborated on a brief fictional notice alluding to the Men in Black, published as fact first in Raymond A. Palmer's Flying Saucers magazine and some of Barker's publications. In the story, Sherwood (writing as "Dr. Richard H. Pratt") claimed he was ordered to silence by the "black men" after learning that UFOs were time-traveling vehicles. Barker later wrote to Sherwood, "Evidently, the fans swallowed this one with a gulp."

Gray Barker's fame spread after his death in 1984 at age 59. A 1995 video by Ralph Coon recognized Barker as one of the 20th century's leading UFO theorists. Barker's collection is now part of the Clarksburg-Harrison Public Library. When asked once if he believed in flying saucers, Barker replied, "I am not sure, but anything that generates that volume of interest is worth collecting."

IN AND OUT OF ZINES

Whatever Happened to Timothy Green Beckley?

As you drive north on New York City's West Side Highway toward the George Washington Bridge the midtown skyscrapers recede and to your right the commerce of downtown blends into vast residential sections. You may get a brief view of Grant's Tomb if you are not preoccupied with dodging angry, fist-shaking drivers.

To your left is the Hudson, lethargic, polluted, and drearily reflecting the lights of the city, reminding one of Poe's "dank tarn of Auber." His darkling lake was located in one of his many enchanted imagination lands, "the ghoul-haunted woodlands of Weir," where the poet searched for his lost Ulalume.

Of course all that is fiction, but tonight George O'Barski, this city will be haunted -- not by ghouls, perhaps, but by something out of space, or out of other time or mind. Tonight, George O'Barski, you will be thrust into that madness.

Across the Hudson, roughly parallelling New York's tangled 80's, you see the rivalling skyline of New Jersey -- dominated by one monstrous structure perched high atop the Palisade Cliffs.

It looks as if it had been thrust upward from the hilltop like a mammoth burrowing cylinder from the Inner Earth. Stonehenge, a cyclopean high-rise apartment building, no doubt is the namesake of the mind-wrenching ruins of England, constructed, nobody knows how, by mysterious antecedents of the heathen residents of pre-Christian Britain. It is two o'clock in the morning and few window lights bedeck the jutting tower of glass and steel. It stands there like some Dark Tower out of Childe Harold's fear, or Keel's Babel.

For the past thirty of your eighty-two years you have made this trip almost nightly. You have closed your small liquor store in Chelsea at midnight and have spent a couple of hours replenishing shelves, reordering and bookkeeping. Now you are making your long trek back to your home in New Jersey.

Across the river you decide to take a detour through North Hudson Park, a huge area, about a fourth as big as New York's Central Park, to avoid the traffic lights of the regular route and to relax in the serenity of this vast area situated on the other side of Stonehenge. Unlike the cutthroat maddness of Central Park, this area is well-policed, and at this hour completely deserted. It is a mild night for January, and you roll down our window to get some fresh air.

As you do so the all-night radio talk show fades and is replaced by static. Then you hear a droning, screeching sound, something like a refrigerator, though with exaggerated electronic overtones. Cold fear grips you as you see brilliant lights pacing your car.

The deafening cacophany stops as a circular device, about 30 feet in diameter, suddenly halts and hovers about 10 feet off the ground. It is flat on the bottom, with vertical sides and a dome about eight feet high. You brake and drive very slowly. You are terrified, yet you are inexplicably fascinated by the drama being unfolded, like some dumb show from a bad dream!

GRAY BARKER'S NEWSLETTER is an official publication of the Saucers and Unexplained Celestial Events Research Society (SAUCERS). Not to be confused with parodies such as SAUCER MEWS or THIS NEWSLETTER IS NOT TO BE CONFUSED WITH: SAUCER NEWS. Published irregularly. 6 issues $6.00. Back issues: Nos. 1 & 2 (two pagers) free with sace. 3 & 4 $3.00 each; 5 $1.00. Exchanges with other zines. Published by Saucerian Press, Inc., Box 2228, Clarksburg, WV 26301 U.S. Clippings and other saucerinformation needed. Gray Barker loves Allen H. Greenfield*.
*Platonicaly

Suddenly a ladder is lowered from the machine, and ten, maybe twelve little figures, about the size of small children, scurry down it. You can't see their faces, which are covered with helmets. They are dressed in uniform-like coveralls, of light color. Their movements are precise and speedy. Like a horde of cosmic carpetbaggers they dig at the ground and scoop up turf and dirt which they toss into bags they carry. They run back up the ladder which retracts like an airline stairway and the machine takes off rapidly with the same high-pitched whining that heralded its arrival, and a new burst of static on the radio.

You still drive slowly, shaken, confused. What is happening? Is the world coming to an end? Have you seen something you shouldn't have seen -- maybe a Government experiment? You reach in the back seat and grab a minature bottle of Old Grand Dad you are taking home as a joke present for a friend. You start to tear the seal and then you stop. You remember you are a teetotaler and that you haven't taken a drop of liquor in more than twenty years. You toss the bottle back into the rear seat.

You realize that the radio, and the talk show has come back on, and in the next block you see the lights of your habitual eating place -- the Fort Lee Diner. But this morning you pass it by, for you cannot think of eating. Normally you would have a good meal and then stay up for a few hours, listening to the radio and walking the dog. but the terror, that for some unexplained reason you did not feel during the awful encounter, now wells up from within you and your hands shake at the wheel. Your only thought is getting home, jumping into bed and pulling the covers over your head!

Sightings Continue

It is ironic that the spectacular sighting took place within a mile of where former UFO investigator James W. Moseley may have been sleeping, at his residence in Cliffside, N. J., during that very hour. Nor was any other UFO buff aware of the mid-January, 1975, landing until the details appeared in an excellently researched and well-written article in THE VILLAGE VOICE by reporter Budd Hopkins (VILLAGE VOICE, 80 University Place, New York, NY 10003. Send $1.80 to Back Issue Dept. if you wish a copy). It is understandable why nobody heard about it earlier -- O'Barski told nobody about his experience. Finally, after a year of silence, he felt he had to tell somebody and confided in reporter Hopkins who had been a regular customer for more than 17 years. Hopkins revisited the site with O'Barski and MUFON investigators and immediately found confirmation of the sighting: remains of the holes the little creatures had dug, though they had been filled in by the park custodian. Further checking disclosed a much more dramatic confirmation: a doorman at Stonehenge had witnessed the same landing, though at a greater distance; as the thing took off a large plate glass window had shattered, as if a projectile had been fired through it.

Hopkins was ready to file his story when he heard of a new development. On January 15, 1976 (about a year to the day after O'Barski's experience -- the witness was not certain of the exact January, 1975 date) employees of Stonehenge reported another and similar landing in the park.

After publication of the VOICE article other reports surfaced. In February people reported that they had seen a mysterious figure wandering in the park. Witnesses described the figure as about five feet tall and wearing something like a miner's helmet with a light coming from it. The being seemed to avoid the street lights and walked in a halting, bounding, robot-like manner, pausing now and then as if picking up something from the ground.

A seven-year-old boy told his parents that on January 29 he saw a saucer-shaped craft with spindly legs land in the park during broad daylight, about 4:30 P.M. A woman who lives a few blocks from Moseley Manor (Moseley owns the apartment house in which he lives) reported seeing low-level flying discs in January and February.

Moseley's "Comeback"

In my No. 3 NEWSLETTER I predicted that James W. Moseley would soon begin publishing a zine, and hinted that he would be getting back into the UFO action. Our predictions were ignored, like the pitiful wailings of the prophetess Cassandra whose curse was never being believed. Like the dire debacles which befel Greece, when that nation did not heed the warnings, we now have visited upon us a publication titled THIS NEWSLETTER IS NOT TO BE CONFUSED WITH SAUCER NEWS (PO Box 163, Ft. Lee, NJ 07024) a 4-pager put out by Moseley. I wasn't entirely right when I predicted he would bring out something really slick, but give him a few more issues.

Either this is a free publication or Jim forgot to mention the subscription price -- though he does indicate, "Back issues available at $0.00 per copy, if we like you." Perhaps this is going to be available only to a favored few. In this issue which he designates as Vol. 23, No. 17 (pretty confusing unless I just haven't been getting previous issues) he reproduces an unsigned letter, allegedly from myself to him, but the bulk of the issue is devoted to excellent coverage of the saucerevents that came after the publication of the VOICE article.

The latter coverage relates some details of what some researchers have termed "a UFO debacle," an event which may be a hopeful harbinger of the resurrection of the Eastern UFO Establishment, with all of that institution's wacky, freewheeling and **democratic** search for Saucertruth. Reading Moseley's issue gives us a feeling akin to seeing an old newsreel of Al Smith leading a convention in singing "Happy Days Are Here Again!". It sets Serious Saucer Investigation back at least six months.

But the main plus factor of the so-called "UFO Debacle" was the resurfacing of a well-known UFO writer/reporter/investigator among the ranks of the New York saucer set. I had supposed that Timothy Green Beckley had "gone underground" after the 1967 NY Flying Saucer Convention, but I was only partly correct.

Beckley had been a notable "teen saucerer" in the 1960's, and for some years had issued a zine called "SEARCHLIGHT". Later Beckley wrote and edited books for my Saucerian Press, such as The Shaver Mystery and the Inner Earth, The Subterranean World, and Timothy Green Beckley's Book of Space Brothers. But I hadn't heard from Bro. Beckley in years and presumed he had given up on UFOs for some sort of prosaic workaday job in New York.

Taking advantage of the renewed New York interest because of the VOICE article and the ensuing sighting wave, Beckley turned up as a full-fledged publicist and literary agent. And he had a client on hand to take advantage of the flap. He and his associate Harold Salkin were representing Chicago radio personality Warren Freiberg, and his wife, Libby, a trance medium. Beckley/Salkin announced that at midnight Saturday, March 6, they and their clients would hold a vigil in the park on the site of the saucer landing, and that Mrs. Freiberg would attempt to contact the occupants after going into a trance.

Moseley consented to allow Beckley/Salkin and the Freibergs to hold a press conference in his apartment (since it was near the sighting location) just prior to the attempted contact, though this was against his better judgment. He knew that a local MUFON chapter had investigated the original landing and considered it authentic; and the medium business might not set well with "serious" UFO people he was trying to relate with.

And Moseley did not reckon with Beckley's ability to get space in leading New York and Jersey papers, as well as the electronic media. As a result of the extensive media coverage prior to the seance, a crowd of at least five hundred people, along with many MUFON members and well-known NY saucerenthusiasts turned up at midnight at Stonehenge.

Beckley, Salkin, Moseley, Eugene Steinberg and a few others formed a circle around the Freibergs as they stood on the landing site. The medium insisted that the circle join her in chanting, "ALPHA! OMEGA!" over and over again. As they did this the crowd, mainly teenagers out for a good time, became surly and unruly.

"ALPHA! OMEGA!" Moseley and the others continued to chant, and then shout, over the noise of the crowd, which, in turn, began shouting and chanting: "FRISBEE! FRISBEE!"

The unruly crowd moved closer, threatening to break the circle, causing Beckley to fear that his clients might be harmed or that there might be a riot,

Fortunately a new "sighting" saved the day (or night): in the distance a little creature, clad in metallic clothing and carrying a flare, attracted the crowd's attention (Moseley, with typical skepticism, insists in his NEWSLETTER that it was a child or midget dressed in tinfoil), and the Freibergs were temporarily abandoned. They seized this opportunity to jump into an automobile, but part of the crowd spotted them, rushed toward them and started pounding on the car and rocking it. The Freibergs, along with Beckley/Moseley et al probably were lucky thus to escape to the Stonehenge lobby with their lives and limbs. The management allowed them to continue the seance on the rooftop of the highrise.

(I recently managed to reestablish contact with Beckley and here is part of his letter describing what ensued):

"Briefly, Libby was put into trance on the roof of the Stonehenge Apartment. An entity who identified himself as Cauldon came through and said that they were in New Jersey to warn us of the misuse of our environment. He said that our environment is their environment, indicating, perhaps, that they exist in another dimension. Cauldon stated further that there would be a sighting over Times Square on the fourth of July.

"Jim didn't take Cauldon's message seriously. Freiberg tried several times to explain to him that quite often low astral spirits can take over a person's body and pretend to be more highly evolved beings (such as space masters). In any event, this was a serious attempt at contacting UFOnauts. It was not a three ring circus as Jim reported in his ego sheet. I understand Dr. J. Allen Jynek has requested a copy of the tape that was made of the otherworldy seance.

"I always did like Moseley, but some times his thoughts are hard to figure out. We recently got together, while investigating the landing reports in New Jersey. My impression was that Jim was not too happy with the attention he got. Thanks to our excellent press relations, the local media played up the appearance of the Freibergs. I think that Jim was sorry he had taken part. As you probably know, when it comes to the occult, Moseley was never too keen. He just hasn't a grasp on what's going on in this area. I've seen him shy away at even getting his Tarot cards read."

Moseley, obviously trying to make a "comeback" in Ufology, adds a disclaimer in his NEWSLETTER: "We apologize to whoever is left in serious 'middle Ufology' for our relatively small part in this fiasco, but we feel it might have been a worthwhile attempt at communication had it been handled differently."

Beckley evidently is doing very well, both professionally and financially. He and Salkin head a firm called Global Communications at 303 Fifth Ave., Suite 1306, New York, NY 10016, AC 212-MU5-4080 (interestingly in the same building as the old Saucer News office during Moseley's heyday). Beckley continues to write UFO material under his own name for publications such as UFO REPORT (a recent article was "Mind Manipulation, the New UFO Terror Tactic").

"Long ago I gave up publishing zines (Beckley writes). I found it was an ineffective way to reach a large number of people (as well as being highly non-profitable). I've turned my attention to the large circulation publications. Since the writer's by-line does not always appear on stories, you probably don't realize that I am contributing a great deal of UFO and psychic material which appears in THE NATIONAL ENQUIRER, NATIONAL STAR, TATTLER, etc. In fact, we just got an extra bonus for our headline story in the ENQUIRER on the Army helicopter that was followed by a UFO over Stockton, California. You might also watch for the July issue of GENESIS.

My story, "Blowing the Lid Off the Great UFO Conspiracy," will be the first saucer article to appear in a quality men's magazine since PLAYBOY did a story more than six years ago. Speaking of PLAYBOY, I just got a call from their Chicago office today. It seems they're working on a story about UFOs to appear late summer."

Beckley, of course, is much more mature (and a trifle more cynical) than during those early days when I may have been one of his minor heros. After Moseley once reported on my beer-drinking habits, Beckley wrote him an angry letter accusing him of slandering me, and I will always like him for that (later, after the NY and other conventions, I doubt that either Beckley or myself can dare to defend each other's intake of foamy grog).

Beckley, along with his successes at writing, publicity, etc., has one distinction I had almost forgotten about, and this is pointed out by Moseley in his article in yet another new zine. CROSSROADS (1471 Second Ave., Apt. 19, New York, N.Y.) is notable because it is co-edited by Geneva Steinberg (our favorite Ufological girlfriend, next to Laura of course), and contributed to by members of the old CAVEAT EMPTOR crowd, such as Eugene Steinberg, Curt Sutherly, and Moseley. The copy I have claims to be a "non-issue," being designated "Vol. 0, No. 0" and with no price designated -- apparently an introductory issue.

It combines saucers, occult, The Old Religion and the like, and the chief editor is a person known only as "Thor". (We doubt this is the "Valiant Thor" of Stranges' chronicles). Moseley's article is particularly witty when he recounts the many saucerzines that have come and gone. He points out that they start out small with one or two pages and gradually grow. When they get to be of excessive size their publishers can no longer support them, either financially or time-wise, and the zines fold, leaving a lot of subscribers holding the bag. He even relates the story of one zine publisher who folded before his first issue came out! Although the publisher is not named, no doubt this is Timothy Green Beckley's ill-fated ESP MAGAZINE which unfortunately did not get off the ground as a professionally edited newsstand publication.

"People still say to me (Beckley told me during a recent phone conversation) that they have read ESP and thought it was a wonderful magazine, although not a single issue was published."

Another Folding

UFOLOGICAL THOUGHTS AND IDEAS (PO Bx 696, Defiance, Ohio 43512), a fine zine edited by Robert S. Easley, has announced it will join the great saucer club in the sky after the present number. Easley will devote his time and talents to assisting Rick Hilberg with his UFO MAGAZINE NEWS BULLETIN (3403 West 119th St., Cleveland, Ohio 44111, 4-ish $2.00). Easley's UTAI No. 9 Febish 76 should be valuable to any serious UFO buff who would like a digest of cases where AF planes have tried to intercept or attack UFOs. An article in that number looks as if it may be a rather complete list of such incidents, and anybody building a research library should have thish on file. No price is given but you should send sace and a buck if possible.

If you've tried to unsuccessfully phone MUFON critics such as Greenfield, Stenberg, Schiller and Moseley, that's because they're hiding out in the bathroom secretly reading SKYLOOK, The UFO Monthly (26 Edgewood Drive, Quincey, Il. 62301, $8 yrly, $9 For. This for sub only, not MUFON membership). Zine is still very much alive after I predicted folding in Threish (Dwight Connelly is catching up and Febish was received the first of March). This zine always has been good, from the days of its mimeo or offset typescript days. When Dwight took this over from first editor Norma Short I thought that it suffered a bit in content with the slick, professional look he gave it. But is it my second childhood, or is this zine getting a lot better lately. I have liked the last couple of ishes very much. 99ish (!!!!!) contains a great report on two occupants spotted in a craft, a report on mysterious helicopters in California which is reminiscent of Keel's Mystery Planes; and a case with an unusual twist: A gal has her car motor stopped by the usual EM, but then the saucerians start up the motor again with the car in low gear!

But it is hairy monster man Stan Gordon (Dir. Pennsylvania Center for UFO Research) who comes up with a real GEM: A Pa. couple living in a mobile home notice a weird little 8-inch disc hovering about their domicile. The housewife is disturbed by the intruder and, catching it hovering low, takes a swat at it with her broom. The saucer breaks into two identical parts, each flying off in a different direction. When Dwight runs stuff like this, Greenfield, he can't be all bad!

SKYLOOK is using more drawings and art work, which is improving its appearance, and even uses a cartoon in the currentish which gives zine a warmer tone; and at the risk of Connelly's excommunication, I'd venture to say there's a Middle-Ufologish feel to thish. From his editorial disclaimer to remarks the editor has made, I gather that Dwight is developing an image for SKYLOOK which is relatively independent from MUFON, which still provides a subscription automatically with membership. The exact relationships, in fact, between the zine and org, are rather hazy and ill-defined.

The editor is doing another great thing: Like Ronald Reagan who broke the rules to critize another Republican candidate, editorial matter in SKYLOOK recently has broken the unspoken rules of the current UFO Establishment and has been mildly critical of other Establishment figures, such as J. Allen Hynek.

Connelly gave this sacred cow an editorial kick in the pants when Hynek invited 138 persons to attend a "secret" "State of UFO Research" meeting scheduled for April 30-May 2 at the Lincolnwood Hyatt House in Chicago (watch for Greenfield to infiltrate this one in his Charlie Hickson suit!). As Connelly pointed out, Hynek made a blunder by sending each invitee a printed list of those privileged elect who made the Roll by virtue of their "track records."

Immediately Xerox stock shot up several points as most of the One Hundred Thirty Eight began dropping dimes in PO machines or freeloading on office copiers. We zine publishers could save a lot of money by printing just one issue of our crud, and sending it out to one fairly active saucerenthusiast. For immediately the phones start buzzing and the Xeroxes cranking when something new (especially something controversial) hits a dedicated Ufologist's mailbox. Then the three people he contacts contact three others each, and there it goes like a chain reaction. My threeish somehow reached Lou Farish's scrutiny in such a roundabout way before any subscribers got it (he's now on my freebie list -- and, Lou, your copy of GIANT CROCK finally went out to you).

Of course this invite was great ego for the One Hundred and Thirty-Eight, but a sure demonstration of How To Lose Friends and Alienate all the OTHER People. In the currentish Dwight notes that the meeting is now termed "closed" but not secret, and that the original list of invitees is being expanded -- but Hynek has already become the victim of his Dale Carnegie twist.

In an excellent followup to the Travis Walton abduction, SKYLOOK dares to headline, "APRO, NICAP, GSW REPORTS DISAGREE," and gives both negative and positive coverage to the Walton case, including an indirect slam at the CAP.

An important UFO organizational news item is a letter from John Schuessler, deputy director of MUFON, to Walter Andrus, Director, announcing the former's resignation.

The full reasons for the Schuessler resignation, though supposedly made clear in the letter, are still hazy in this reporter's head: He avers he is not hushed up, nor has he had any dispute with the MUFON heirarchy. There has been no pressure from his employer or family.

"The accumulation of things leading to my decision was culminated by the forthcoming CUFOS symposium in April (Hynek's 'secret' meeting -- see above -- GB)." Schuessler received an invitation and assumed that Andrus had pulled the brass on Hynek to get him in -- then he was dismayed to find out that Andrus had nothing to do with the invite, and evidently knew little about the **meeting!** We can't be certain, but we assume that Andrus, himself, was not invited! Here is the Deputy Director getting invited to Hynek's **Meeting** of the Elect, and then learning that the Director may not have been invited and has expressed dismay at the meeting. "I felt as if I had shirked a duty by not making sure you (Andrus) was informed." Schuessler gets the December SKYLOOK and notes that Hynek is the featured speaker for the June MUFON symposium (After Hynek had remarked that such symposiums (should we say **symposia?**) were "unprofessional").

The Schuessler letter than goes into a general discussion involving the witholding of UFO information by individuals and groups and their refusing to share it, all of which, again, sounds a bit hazy and persecuted. And the resignee is greatly upset by the inclusion of author Phil Klass on the recent Arkansas UFOtroika program, and the lionization by several people present at the Fort Smith affair.

Klass, according to Schuessler, "is a distasteful character that should be placed in the category of gossip columnists."

Regardless of our criticisms of MUFON, or our differences of opinion with SKYLOOK editorial policy, we of Middle Ufology should kick some kudos toward Connelly personally, who has managed to get out a quality publication for months, no doubt involving personal sacrifices. And considering the arithmetic of a roughly 1300 circulation zine selling at 8 bucks a year, Dwight certainly cannot be getting any fun money out of his task. We understand that the editor, who holds down a very demanding and full-time "eating" job, does all the editorial work, including pasting up the layouts. His wife takes care of the mountain of correspondence, collection of subscriptions, and other gruelling paperwork.

That Mr. and Mrs. Connelly are dedicated people in the UFO field there can be no doubt -- nor is there any doubt that if Dwight continues his lively editorial policy we have noted of late, the bathroom doors of more and more MUFON critics will remain locked for even longer periods of time!

A Wisp With a Will

UNKNOWN WORLDS -- THE WISP JOURNAL (c/o WISP--World Investigators of Strange Phenomena, Rt 2, Bx 159, Vina, Al 35593, Mbship $3 US & Can, $5 For., $10 for Air per yr For, bi-monthly and you get extra stuff like membership certificate, sighting forms, etc.) is pubbed by Steven Elliott, assisted by other Elliott brigands incl Ernie O., Mary P. and Lynda. We've seen two nos. of this and both have been extremly good. WISPISH 8 contains Part Two of a Herculian task assumed by Gilbert J. Ziemba which involves a complete (as far as possible) chronology of all UFO sightings. Thish contains sightings from Jan. 10-21/75 which comprise seven of the zine's 24pp. Ziemba is continuing this project despite a tragic situation which befell him wherein all of his personal UFO material was destroyed (In a letter to me he said it wasn't a fire, but seemed reluctant to tell just actually had happened, adding to the mystery). This certainly is a laudable project and one which I hope Ziemba and editor Elliott can sustain, so if you're after a UFO chronology better send off. UW carries an excellent capsule book review section covering UFOs and other subjects the zine covers listed on the masthead, such as Atheism, Buddhism, Confucianism, Cultism, Dogmatism, Existentialism, Extraterrestrialism, Fanatacism, Fundamentalism, Futurism, Geocentrism, Hellenism, Intellectualism, Janism, Mentalism, Occultism, Paganism, Phenomenalism, Psychism, Qabbalism, Spiritualism, Satanism, Saucerism, Taoism, Zoroastrianism, and, to catch most everything else, the editor adds, "and anything else strange, unexplained and unknown."

Book Review

A Disestablishmentarian **Among** the Avante Garde

SAUCERS AND SAUCERERS, by Allen H. Greenfield, P.A.N.P. Press, POB 98214, Briarcliff Branch PO, Atlanta, Ga 30329, 1976, 72 pages, $1.00.

"The establishment once again shows its infinite capacity to absorb its natural enemies, and thus live on, stagnant and hollow though it may be."

So Allen H. Greenfield may be lamenting the near normalization of the once-nutty saucer subject, as it is now accepted by the common man the Nation over, is a staple item in such fine family publications as GRIT and THE NATIONAL ENQUIRER, and is purveyed by pseudo-scientific groups such as APRO and NICAP, with archetypal symbols such as Keyhoe and Adamski abandoned for gurus such as Hynek and maybe, though not quite, Keel.

Greenfield came on the Ufological scene at mid-term during the not-so-fabulous '60's, an interregnum between the Palmers, Mengers, Barkers and other crowned heads of the early days, and todays invasions by the barbarians led by the flag of Academia, annoyed but not halted by guerillas such as Keel.

Though Jim Moseley might have laid some claim to this regency, it bore the escutheon of a phenomenon Greenfield yclepts the "teen saucer movement," that was to give us (in the 70's) the underground of Hilberg, Farish, Clark, Steinberg, Rettig and other notables, now grown up and largely matured, though, even in the radical field of Ufology, still innovating and avante garde.

Teen-saucerer -- now Middle Ufologist Greenfield believes the Old Ufology of the '50's, with its freewheeling contacteeism and extraterrestrial invasions, was essentially a grassroots social phenomenon. Now it has turned into a fringe branch of orthodox science. By the '80's it may become "what we have seen parapsychology become in recent years: not quite orthodoxy, but no longer merely fringe."

Greenfield's haunting memories of the rise of the UFO convention and the Eastern Establishment (a la Moseley) in the '60's is nostalgic and heartwarming to anybody who participated in those golden days. These memories are particularly valuable to the UFO historian, and dominate the second half of S&S. But the first part, consisting of reprinted articles from his various publications, gives the book its stature, and establishes the author as probably today's deepest thinker on what Ufology and UFOs are really about. Unlike Peter Kor, he displays the ability to transform some of his rather abstruse thoughts into communicative prose.

Heretofore these essays have been scattered through the welter of brief-lived publications he has issued (Greenfield's zines, to be filed properly, would require too many file folders for my own system, so I handle them with one big file drawer labeled, "Greenfield, Miscellaneous Publications Of"). Scattered here and there in original source form, the essays have been largely inaccessable except to the most dedicated saucer nut with a bibliographic syndrome. Assembled here by Greenfield in S&S they are not only easily accessible, but assume a surprising sophistication, considering that many of them were written long before his present level of maturity was reached.

Next to "The Myth of Ufology," I believe his most intriguing treatment is a chapter (and an article reprint) titled "What You Should Keep In Mind About The 'Subjective Hypothesis'". If I could deal with this subject here in proper review, I probably could have written S&S, so I urge you to read the book.

Part of my difficulty may be that one grasps the Subjective Hypothesis intuitively, rather than logically. When Greenfield may speak highly of some of my own writings he may be subconsciously realizing that an intuitive approach to the Hypothesis may be present there. Although I may be able to inject this into an article or a book chapter, it is mainly subconscious, and not the sort of thing I could put into an outline.

But let's give it a futile try. In thish you have a Jerome Eden and a Professor Jerome **Greenfield** hung up on Wilhelm Reich, yet disagreeing. Allen H. **Greenfield** and a NYC resident, Allan Greenfield (who sells me old-time **16mm** movie cartoons for my collection), are in the same issue, but at opposite ends of saucer beliefs. In some other ish you might find a Gray **Barker** investigating a case where a saucer has ripped the bark off a tree, or, in Silver Bridge, looking into a case where a **dog** has disappeared, the victim of a giant bird creature. And the owner of the dog is Newell Partridge.

You don't quite know whether these people and situations have been drawn together because of name similarities, acting, psychologically, on their own volitions -- or whether some outside **intelligence** (the saucerians) have **consciously** brought these elements together, or because they simply may be confused. Keel has written about Ufonauts who occasionally are confused about time.

If you are a serious saucer buff and would like to avoid the confusion of reviews such as this one, I urge you to send off $1.00 without delay to the publisher's address above. (If you also enclose the charred remains of a current APRO, MUFON or NICAP membership card -- or a clipped logo from an old Flying Saucers Palmerzine cover of the '60's, I can almost guarantee that you will receive two copies of S&S, along with lifetime subscriptions to Greenfieldzines.)

And should you happen to be illiterate, Bob Hewitt's jacket design, in one overpowering flash of sudden perception, may tell you more about the Solution to the Flying Saucer Mystery than you could ever find in this or other books -- even if you aren't smoking dope.

--Gray Barber

MEETINGS

The 1976 MUFON Conference will take place at Weber's Inn in Ann Arbor, Michigan, Saturday and Sunday, June 12-13. Speakers on Saturday will include Jacques Vallee and J. Allen Hynek, Henry McKay, Dave Webb, William Spaulding, and Ray Stanford. Sunday afternoon will feature workshops on investigative techniques. Advance registration for all three sessions of the conference and including dinner is $16.00 per person. Send checks (payable to Michigan UFON) to: Bob Stinson, 2903 Sheffield Ct., Ann Arbor, Michigan 48105.

UFO SIGHTINGS NEWSLETTER announces the first Mountain States UFO Believers' Get-Together on August 7-8, 1976. Place: Guanella Pass Campgrounds, 8 miles south of Georgetown, Colorado. Bring your camper. Registration fee per person $2.00 cash. Those not sending cash must make MO's payable only to: Janice M. Croy, 512 S. Logan, Denver, Co 80209. Free map of area on request. Saucer sighting(s) almost guaranteed out thar in the wilds!

COVER: Cartoonist Fred L. Gresham depicts dilemna of James W. Moseley, to illustrate the Biblical verses: "Behold, ye shall be weighed in the balance and found wanting." and "Judge not, lest ye be judged" (sic).

THIS ISSUE delayed, due to persecutions, mainly financial.

GRAY BARKER'S NEWSLETTER not to be confused with NEW SAUCERS or SAUCER CRUISE.

FOR SALE: SIMULATED SAUCER. Be the first in your block to create a real scare. Breaks down quickly and packs in ordinary station wagon for fast getaway. Glows in many colors and provides simulated radiation effect. Built-in static generator creates radio and TV interference in one-mile radius. Will not fly and is not to be confused with CIA models. Set up saucer beside a road and watch for fast results! Then be first on the scene to "investigate" the sighting and get fat interviews with newspapers and big-time UFO researchers. Apply c/o NEWSLETTER prices and delivery dates.

Letters

Dear Mr. Barker:

Received your March, 1976, "Newsletter," and was glad to see that you are able to make contact with Wilhelm Reich's work after nearly twenty years. Perhaps there is still some hope for mankind, but I am far from optimistic at this late stage in the game. Without Reich's genius and guiding hand, humanity lost its greatest pro-Life scientist. You forgot that Dr. Eva Reich begged you to testify at her father's trial, and you refused (You stated as much in your letter published in FATE magazine in 1960 or 1961 -- I am sure you will recall that incident now).

We all failed Reich, however; and in failing him we may very well have sealed our fate.

At least you tried to be objective and stick to the facts, which is more than can be said for John Keel and others who refuse even to study Reich; although more and more ufologists and scientists are being forced by events to read Reich's great books instead of making contemptuous, irrational statements because of their fear and arrogance. Aside from the minor errors in your account, let's focus on a few major points you either glossed over or omitted entirely:

You state (p. 5), "The Federal Drug Administration ended a long investigation by seeking a court order to prevent Reich from employing his ORACCU for the treatment of disease...." There never was "a long investigation" of Reich in any scientific sense. There never was a bonafide attempt on the part of any government agency to actually study Reich's discovery of the cosmic and biological orgone energy. Never! The entire FDA "investigation" was a fraud in the first place. This is thoroughly documented in Jerome Greenfield's book, Wilhelm Reich Vs. The USA (W. W. Norton, N. Y., 1974). The fact that all of Reich's works published in English were ordered banned and burned (including many books that have absolutely nothing to do with the discovery of the orgone) indicates what motivate the assault against Reich. Who bans and burns scientific, sociological and psychological literature on this planet? What is at stake here is not only Reich's "freedom" of scientific inquiry and "free speech" -- but also your freedom and my freedom to think, to investigate, and to publish.

Where Professor Greenfield and I part company, however, is where he opines that Reich's UFO interests and beliefs indicate he went nuts! Greenfield states, for example, that the US Air Force was never seriously interested in Reich's UFO research. My research (see "Reich's Contact With the U. S. Air Force," EDEN BULLETIN, 2:4. p. 2) **proves** by factual evidence that the Air Force was keenly interested in Reich's UFO research, particularly in his disabling of UFOs in Maine, and later in Tucson, Arizona.

You state (p. 6) "Eden creates his own Reichenese." I can assure you, the majority of the terms I use in my book, Planet In Trouble, were coined by Reich, not me. And I see nothing wrong in it -- nothing wrong in calling an orgone-energy accumulator an "orac (Don't you call a "magazine" a zine?) -- or in calling Hoodlums in Government "HIGs".

"You say further (p. 6) "Reich was not able to communicate well with his associates and the scientific comunity at large." That he was able to so communicate is proven by the many scienfidic articles published by more than a score of highly accredited physicians and scientists both here and abroad. In my book, **Orgone Energy** -- The Answer to Atomic Suicide, I list the names, credentials and affiliation of some 20 of these scientists **and physicians** who wrote and published scientific papers attesting to the validity of Reich's discovery of a pre-atomic, mass-free energy.

Furthermore, you failed to mention that since 1967, a scientific journal of the highest caliber has been publishing additional papers and articles by additional physicians and scientists who are today continuing to validate and enlarge upon Reich's astounding discoveries. That publication is The Journal of Orgonomy, Box 565, Ansonia Station, New York, N.Y. 10023, edited by my friend Elsworth F. Baker, M.D., an outstanding physician, psychiatrist and medical orgone therapist.

Now if the "scientific" community refuses to read, to seriously study, and to duplicate Reich's basic experimental data (given for example in his basic book, The Cancer Biopathy), whose fault is that? If UFOlogists in general are so frightened of truth and fact, of the documented data and published findings of Reich.......who then is responsible for the "lack of communication" as you term it.

The invasion of Earth's atmosphere by UFOs is an extremely serious and frightening matter. It should be front-page, daily news. The additional facts (evidenced by Reich and myself) that UFOs may indeed be hostile, that they are engaged in a kind of planetary warfare unknown to Earthmen, that they are using the practically limitless power of orgone energy in our universe -- all of these additional facts make the situation even more pregnant with disaster.....unless Mankind wakes up, faces its terrors, and begins to shoulder the burdens and responsibilities that UFOs and Reich's research indicate. If these same arrogant and terrified Little Men were Zapped by a UFO light beam, as I was, and sent to bed for a week with radiation sickness, they would be "laughing" out of a lower part of their anatomy! And now we are further confronted with a world-wide wave of UFO- associated cattle mutilations, thoroughly documented, as you know, in my EDEN BULLETIN.

As you know, Mr. Barker, I have spent a great deal of time, effort, and my own money in attempting to bring some of the facts regarding Whilhelm Reich's UFO research before public scrutiny. My motive is neither publicity, money, nor power; it is simply survival! I ask you to help me, to help yourself and your loved ones, and to help all Life on our planet. We need good, responsible people who understand the importance of Reich's work and who are seriously willing to work for Life.

Sincerely yours, Jerome Eden (Box 34, Careywood, Idaho 83809)

Dear Mr. Eden:

As you will recall, during our telephone conversation I mentioned that I either had not refused Eva Reich's request to testify at her father's trial, or had completely forgotten such a matter. At that time you could not recall the issue of FATE that carried such a letter. I believe you are wrong -- perhaps some reader can locate the letter -- if indeed there were one. I did not intend to say that you created the "Reichenese" I listed in the glossary. I meant to convey that you had created one of the terms, "HIGs." Perhaps this also was coined by Reich. I personally feel that the "Reichenese" (a "Barkenese" term I coined myself) is colorful and makes your books more readable and communicative. I think your checking will reveal that Keel has dealt with Reich (though perhaps briefly) in books and magazine articles. Your publisher, Exposition Press, just send me a copy of your latest book, Animal Magnetism, about the work of Dr. Mesmer. It is strange, but I always thought of Mesmer as some sort of stage hypnotist or entertainer until I skimmed through your book. That shows how lack of knowledge can distort a subject, and no doubt Reich has suffered similarly. Your objections to my brief coverage of Reich are few, so I'll give myself a pat on the back for handling this complex subject reasonably well. My own personal opinion is 50/50 that Reich was either a wild raving nut -- or a genius far ahead of his time. Incidentally I once learned that a movie, "W. R. -- The Mystery of the Organism," was filmed and shown in a few selected theatres. When I inquired about it, however, the distributor told me it had been withdrawn from circulation because the film prints were worn out or damaged. This doesn't make sense because I don't think the film was ever shown widely. Can you or any reader give us a brief review of this film? -- G.B.

Dear Gray:

I must strongly object to the placement of me by John Keel on the far right of his UFO opinion spectrum. I have never stated or believed that the only explanation for UFOs is estraterrestrial spacecraft. What I have said over and over again is "The evidence is overwhelming that planet Earth is being visited by intelligently controlled vehicles from off the earth. In other words some UFOs are somebody else's spacecraft." I don't rule out 4th dimensional time travellers, popping in and out. I simply find no reason for jumping to that conclusion when there is so much evidence indicating that SOME UFOs are three dimensional objects showing up on radar and on camera film, producing definite physical changes in the earth and vegetation where they land. Ted Phillips' latest compilation of physical trace cases now includes more than 913 cases from 46 countries. Roughly 1/4 of these cases involve reports of critters associated with the craft sitting on or near the ground.

I know that John and many other jumpers to multidimensional solutions for UFOs are under the false impression that trips between stars are impossible. This notion is simply untrue. There are published studies by reputable engineers in excellent technical journals clearly indicating that trips to nearby stars are indeed feasible with round trip times shorter than 60 years and without violating the laws of physics and using staged fission and fusion propulsion systems on both of which I have worked as an industrial nuclear physicist.

Even if the vehicles observed here pop through space and time from some other solar system rather than using fission or fusion systems, that in no way changes my initial statement that some UFOs are spacecraft from some other solar system.

It would frankly amaze me if advanced aliens didn't use techniques of what we call parapsychology. This surely doesn't mean that everything about them is parapsychological rather than physical. One would have to expect that advanced aliens know a great deal of technology with which we are not at all familiar. After all, any study of the development of more and more sophisticated technology indicates that technological progress comes from doing things differently in an unpredictable way.

Perhaps I should also stress that because my professional background is in the development of advanced nuclear and space systems I have focussed on the area of ufology most relevant to my expertise. I cannot claim to be an expert on mythology, ancient archeology, or even parapsychology so I leave those aspects to the people who are. I do know much about technology. I only wish that those who opt for multi-dimensional non-physical explanations for all UFOs would get familiar with the technical literature that abounds. After all in my papers I have loads of references. People do not need to take my word for things. They can look up the references. I would be happy to send a free list of scientific items to anyone sending me a self addressed stamped envelope to POB 502, Union City, CA 94587.

Hastily, Stan (Stanton T. Friedman, 31628 Trevor Avenue, Hayward, Ca 94544) (Keel's opinion spectrum was in our No. 5 -- G.B.)

Dear Gray,

I received your Newsletter (No. 5) and I must truly say that Mr. Duplantier's sketches really fascinated me as well as mentally recalling for me an experience which touches my soul and inner thoughts very deeply! You and your staff did and an excellent job and I appreciate it very much.

The MIB you mentioned in my case may very well have been the CIA or other Federal Authorities. But I cannot understand why they would question me about bizarre situations and information such as they did.

I had another MIB-type experience recently. Since I do research in rocketry, from time to time I experiment with both solid and liquid fuel formulâs. Just the other night one or more persons broke into my study and stole small quantities of almost every compound. They messed up and spilled some nitrocellulose on the ground outside my house. If this were the MIB, it seems they are now taking to Chinese fireworks!

I apologize for seeming so "clammed up" and elusive during our interview, however this was necessary and I will explain later. Perhaps when we meet again I can discuss some other data which I have been holding from conversation. It isn't that I was trying to lie to you, I was just trying to "get the feel" of your basis of approach to the UFO problem before being completely open with you. But you hit the nail on the head when you sensed the horror of UFO activity and encounters with entities which I have had and which still troubles me greatly. I had hoped it hadn't showed.

Most sincerely, Jennings (Jennings H. Frederick, Rt. 1, Box 126, Rivesville, WV 26588.)

Dear Mr. Barker,

Program resumes. Will write you again 17 May.

Will telephone you 16 August at 3:00 P.M., 1976. Thank you.

Respectfully yours, Michael A. Generelli, Jr., UFO News Committee, 483 West View Place, Fairview, NJ 07022.

Dear Sir:

You might tell Mr. Keel that he shouldn't complain about Vallee and others "stealing" his ideas. "His" ideas are merely rehashes of Peter Kor's original work published in the 1950s and 1960s.

C. Keller, c/o 11384 Auburn Rd., Chardon, O 44024

Dear Gray;

Methinks the guy who encountered the "vegetable man" wrote to me sometime back during a period when I wasn't answering much mail. I recall his description of his mother's sighting but he didn't mention the other stuff. I have intriguing correspondence from at least two others who had strange UFO experiences just before entering the Air Force...and they both wound up in Intelligence work! The encounter with the vegetable man was probably a confabulation to cover up what actually happened when he was put into a trance state and injected...or had blood removed. He might have been programmed at that time for a future event, something that happened while he was in the service. Later he was deprogrammed by the MIB. OR the later MIB incident was an attempt to find out what he had been programmed to do during the vegetable man episode.

I recall an old movie starring Frank Gorshin and made circa 1958 in which UFOs landed and creatures very similar to vegetable man used their long fingernails to inject alcohol into their victims. Can't remember the name of the flick but it seemed to be based on a real incident.

Don't use my remark about Jerome Eden. The poor guy is hypersensitive and he will be forever enraged. Just note, if you must, that I have mentioned Reich frequently in my august works.

Poor Moseley. He once begged to join Specialized Research but I had to turn him down. He couldn't pass our basic literacy test. Being refused membership in MUFON is like being refused admittance to a Leper colony. I think he has a notable track record...rejected by MUFON and NICAP, hated by Coral Lorenzen and APRO, humiliated by Joe Pyne. All he needs now is a character endorsement from Richard Nixon to make his triumph complete.

I haven't seen Hynek's secret list but I heard about the secret meeting about two days after he decided to hold it. I hear he was in town for the big Star Trek convention a few weeks back....right in his element. He is still crying for an angel to give him funds....after being turned down by every respectable foundation in the country. The National Enquirer has been sponsoring his UFO CENTER and thus monopolizing whatever reports he manages to collect. (Hynek has recently withdrawn from his association with that publication -- G.B.) I suppose he would pose for

SUNSHINE & HEALTH playing volleyball if they offered him some money.

You sue Moseley for a few million....then I will sue you....and Hynek will sue me....and the wealth will get spread around.

Stendek, -jakeel (John A. Keel, Box 351, Murray Hill Station, New York, NY 10016)

Dear Mr. Barker,

I have just read 'GRAY BARKER'S NEWSLETTER' and although it is very informative, I am firmly convinced that all UFO sightings are either the result of (a) hallucinations (b) natural phenomena or (3) publicity stories made up by individuals who are seeking attention. I believe that all the money being spent on UFO investigations should be channeled into other areas such as cancer research, political funding, or sex education.

Sincerely, A.G. (Allan Greenfield, 170 West 23rd St., New York, NY 10011).

Dear Gray:

I have just read the "rave" review of your publication, Gray Barker's Newsletter, in Al Greenfield's Ufology Notebook. I would appreciate it greatly if you would send me a copy (#4). If you offer subscriptions, information regarding that would be welcome. Do you still sell UFO books & publications?

Thanking you, Dale Rettig, 3233 Buchanan St., San Francisco, Ca 94123.

Dear Dale,

Booklist is enclosed. While I question Al's literary tastes, I certainly will defend to the death his right to publish such comments. Incidentally, we are talking about Allen H. Greenfield, or Atlanta, Ga., and not his anti-UFO near-namesake in New York writing above, Gray.

Dear Gray,

I thought I told you at the time about the "funny thing" that happened while Jim and I visited you some years ago, and which I mentioned in my letter published in Ufology Notebook. But anyhow, here is what I referred to in my letter:

The day we stopped off to see you, you weren't in at first, and so we wandered across the street to grab a bottle of pop at the little grocery store which was so convenient. While drinking the soda we asked the grocer if he had any idea of where you might be, and he said no. But then he told us this story about how a couple of weirdos in black suits had visited your pad one day while you were away for a weekend. They had, he said, wandered about the property, peered into windows, etc., and finally left.

Jokingly, the grocer said, "Maybe they were 'aliens' looking for Mr. Barker." Sounded (and still does) pretty MIBish to me.

Sincerely, Xerox (Curt Sutherly, Box 225, Fredericksburg, Pa. 17026.)

Dear "Xerox", The grocer never did mention this to me. Would ask him about it, but that was sometime back and the clerks come and go. Your letter reminds me of a kid who used to mow lawns in the neighborhood. One evening when I returned home he mentioned that somebody had been looking for me, and mentioned it had been a weird little guy dressed in black who had been peering in through my front window! Of course I am entirely skeptical about all these MIB stories. Gray.

Dear Mr. Barker:

In regard to MIPRO assisting you in MIB cases in Michigan, we would be delighted in assisting you all we can. However, I should point the part in my original letter to which I underlined, in regard to my age.

Being 14, I find that few adults take me seriously when I tell them about MIPRO. And although I am dead serious, I am often restricted from investigating things I would like to by my age and financial status.

Yours truly, Charles Blackburn (Michigan Phenomena Research Organization, 10355 Bird Road, Dowling, Mich. 49050.)

Dear Charles:

You probably are referring to one major UFO organization which, in its printed literature, publicaly discriminates because of (younger) age. If I did not utilize the resources of anybody, regardless of age, I might be neglecting the assistance of somebody with the stature of Max B. Miller, early UFO researcher who started out when he was 12. Or an Allen H. Greenfield, who publishes what probably is the leading UFO "zine" or newsletter in this field. He began, as you are beginning, as a "teen saucerer." So did Dale Rettig, Jerome Clark, Eugene Steinberg, Timothy Green Beckley, and a score of others. They faced your own disadvantages of age and finances, but this did not deter these teenagers from making enormous contributions to UFO research. Gray Barker

Dear Gray,

I enjoyed Newsletter Number Five and predict that it will become a collector's item. The Moseley situation demands an airing. The Vegetable Man article was entertaining and the Reich piece was informative. It's John Keel, however, that causes me to drop you this note.

It not John's rantings about being used by Vallee and Hynek (though he probably is correct) that concerns me. Rather it his schematic diagram of present day Ufology.

John purports to assemble along a right to left continium the various characters in the UFO drama. On the far right would be those committed to the Extraterrestrial Hypothesis (ETH): Contactee cults, NICAP, MUFON, Friedman, Keyhoe). To their near left would be APRO, Blum and Saga who allegedly maintain that the ETH is the "most likely" explanation. To the left of the second group and in the center of the diagram are the Middle Ufologists: Hynek, **Flying Saucer Review**, who supposedly maintain that "all possible explanations should be equally considered." To the left of the Middle Ufologists would be the Conservative Left: The U.S. Government, Menzel, Klass, who dismiss UFOs as misunderstood natural events. Finally, to the extreme left appear the "Radical Left': Creighton, Vallee, Keel and Clark, who reject the ETH in favor of an alternative explanation -- that UFOs are in reality the products of an environmental mechanism that produces myths and beliefs.

I will not raise issues about the validity of John's characterization of the participants or of the importance of producing a schematic diagram. My objection is that although NICAP and the cults have established a certain orthodoxy in their own subcultural worlds, there is no good reason to use the ETH as a measurement standard. Perhaps John is really talking about who he likes and who he dislikes.

If one were to create a schema to describe Ufology, one would not begin with one deviant belief system and work toward another: There is little reason to believe that the ETH is inherently more "right wing" than the fourth dimensional theory which Keel favors. They are both deviant from the persepctive of common sense (Actually many MUFON types are intrigued with the fourth dimension theory; and since Betty Hill, many MUFONers take contactees and abductees quite seriously).

I think that it makes better sense to classify Ufologists by their expressed preference for order -- emotional and intellectual. To do this we would begin with the everyday world, the common sense reality that constitutes a mental "home base" for most people. It includes "obvious" understandings about how the world works. These ideas represent the practical wisdom of everyday people trying to deal with the mundane world. Not included in this belief system are UFOs. The folk beliefs that constitute Common Sense need not be orderly or systematic; they simply work as a receipe works when baking a cake.

The idea that the real world is orderly and systematized belongs to science. Some scientists assume that the scientific model is only a convenient set of helpful assumptions. Others feel that the reality of

UFO, Occult and Metaphysical hobbyists	The Occult Theorists	The Common Sense World	The Worlds of Scientific Theory and UFO **Religions**
Laymen who enjoy the action. Autodidacts who read but do not systematize their knowledge. Anomalies are considered as exciting mysteries for leisure enjoyment rather than serious contemplation.	Independent Researchers who take the existence of UFOs and other anomalies as tentative facts pointing to other realities (ETH, 4th dimension, hollow earth).	People not particularly knowledgeable about the UFO culture. See UFO reports as curiosities or a source of fanciful speculation.	Debunkers who insist that UFOs can be explained as illusions or natural phenomena. Contactees who have absolute knowledge of space people, other worlds, other realities.

>————————**Preference** for intellectual———————————>
and emotional order

theoretical science is the "real reality." Among the latter appear to be the chronic debunkers of alleged anomalies. Interestingly, they are joined in their preference for order by contactees who inevitably encounter space brothers and beautiful space sisters from perfect worlds.

If we place the desire for intellectual and emotional order on a continuum, the debunkers and the contactees stand to the right. Then come the people who take the common sense stance. To their left would be persons who (like Keel but also like ETH proponents) accept anomalies as fact and then attempt to develop deviant theoretical systems to make them sensible.

To the left of the UFO Theorists are those folks who are comfortable with contradictions and ambiguities. These are the followers and the seekers, the people who like the excitement of mysteries. Often they claim to half-believe and hold that various contactees have "part of the truth," and that other occult and metaphysical sources also offer some things of value.

Here is my model in schematic form (See above--GB). Perhaps other readers would like to join the discussion.

Best, Bernard Benign

MEETINGS

MYSTICON '76 presents SAUCERS, SPACE AND SCIENCE FICTION on May 22, 1976, in the Grand Ballroom of the Hospitality Motor In at I-71 and Bagley Road, Middleburg Hts., Ohio (Cleveland suburb). Lectures and slide shows at 7:00 P.M. featuring personalities such as Allan J. Manak, Rick R. Hilberg, Allen H. Greenfield and Robert S. Easley. Admission at door, $2.00.

The Thirteenth Annual NATIONAL UFO CONFERENCE will be held the weekend of August 28, 1976, at the Holiday Inn, Route I-71 and Ohio 82 (Turnpike Exit #10), Strongsville, Ohio. For further information write: Allan J. Manak, Co-Chairman, 5002 Yorkshire Drive, Parma, Ohio 44129. The Conference is an outgrowth of the old Congress of Scientific Ufologists, which, quoting UFOLOGY NOTEBOOK, has, over the years, "ranged from a quiet, academic gathering, to free-wheeling social events, to spectacular pomp and public spectacle."

"STATE OF UFO RESEARCH" meeting, April 30-May 2, Lincolnwood Hyatt House in Chicago. Sponsored by J. Allen Hynek and admittance by invitation only. Subject of considerable controversy (See Page 7). We've been trying to get a copy of this "secret list" of invitees. Won't somebody help ye Editor?

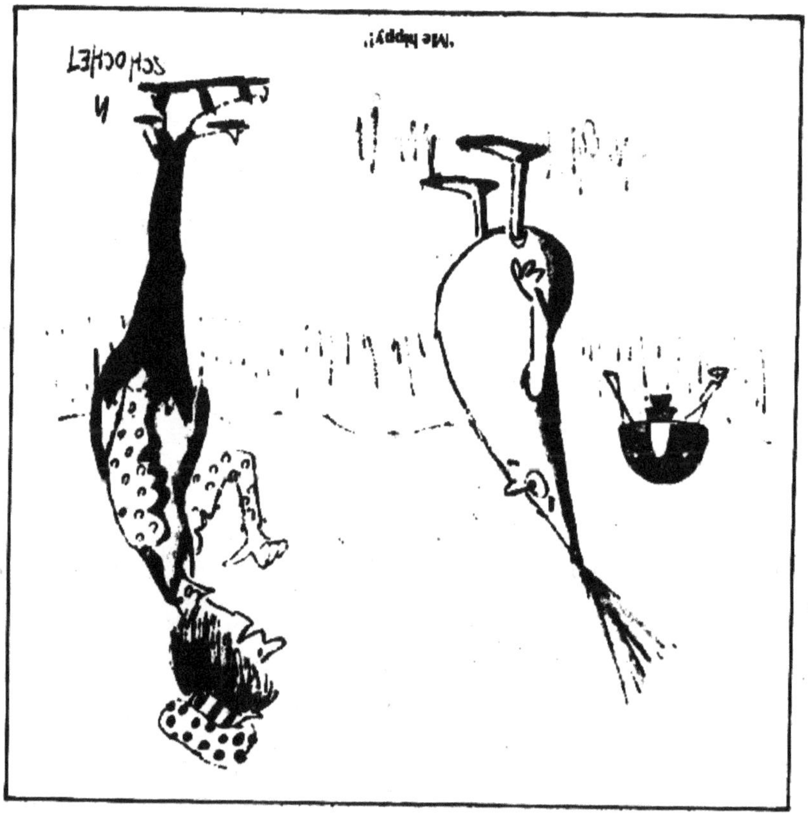

'Me hippy!'

From
Saucerian Press, Inc.
Box 2228
Clarksburg, WV 26301
U.S. Planet Earth

THIRD CLASS MAIL

Postperson, please deliver to:

This issue dedicated
to James Moseley and
George Montgomery.

www.ingramcontent.com/pod-product-compliance
Lightning Source LLC
Chambersburg PA
CBHW050415110426
42812CB00006BA/1898
* 9 7 8 1 9 5 5 0 8 7 4 7 6 *